Capture a life of experiences & memories over 52 weeks

MY DAD SAYS....

Pick one page each week to complete and by the end of the year you'll have a priceless book

You deserve to shine

About
the Book

Pick one numbered page to complete each week

Complete as an activity with family, or
complete alone
Add dates and detail to bring it alive

Some pages and topics will not be relevant to
your life, either alter them slightly or add a
drawing instead

Duplicated prompts are deliberate

There should be something you
can complete on each page...
...At the end of the year you have
a priceless book
to give your children titled

'My Dad Says...'

Also
in the book

There are 5 pages to share with others

- ✶ Complete these pages
- ✶ Take a photo
- ✶ Post in your family chat, or with the hashtag
- ✶ Search the hashtag to see what others shared

You Deserve To Shine

About me

I'm a Mum of 2 children. One boy and one girl, both Teenagers. I'm very lucky.

I've also been lucky with my Dad who has always been kind & positive and I know he would do anything for me, and often still does!

Being a parent is a huge privilege and being able to pass on my thoughts, my memories and my advice is something I treasure.

I hope you will also enjoy passing on some parts of your life that were maybe forgotten, or unknown.

♡ Gillian
xx

How would you describe a Dad?

'A Dad is someone who can give you a view on how to see the difficult things in life coming, and how to avoid them, or if you're too late, how best to deal with them

Louis

'You can always depend on a Dad, he makes you feel safe and will always put you first. He can make you laugh without even trying and occasionally comes out with nuggets of wisdom!'

Caroline

How does a Dad make you feel?

'A Dad makes you feel like you can accomplish anything from riding a bike to passing your driving test. He makes you feel like you are one in a million.

Caroline

'A Dad makes you feel safe, protected, loved and advised in a way only Dads can...

Louis

The world needs more great men
and that starts with great Dads

Gillian

D

Adoptive

Dad
to
be

ill

Teenage

A

Foster

Single

Dementia

This book is for all Dads

D

Discarded

Step

Mute

Bereaved

Contents

My Immediate Family

Me

My Birth Name

Known as ....

My Mum & Dad ....

My Siblings ....

My Cousins ....

....

What I call my Mum's Mum & Dad ....

....

What I call my Dad's Mum & Dad ....

....

Precious Pets

....

....

Me

My Siblings

Their birthdays . . . .

. . . .

I am eldest/middle/youngest/other

Own room/share a room . . . .

Games we played together . . . .

. . . .

Jobs we had around the house . . . .

. . . .

Siblings friends

. . . .

. . . .

Me

Special memories with
my siblings

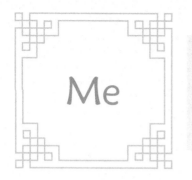

Me

My cousins

Their birthdays ·

Cousins pets ·

Any sleepovers ·

What we did together & with our mutual grandparents ·

· ·

How often we saw each other
· · · · · · · · · · · · · · · · · · · ·

The cousin I am closest to ·

I am the
eldest/middle/youngest
cousin

4/52

Me

Special memories with
my cousins

Me

Their birthdays

Where they lived

How I felt going to visit

How often we saw them

Any sleepovers

Any pets

The games we played

The places we went

I am their
eldest/middle/youngest
grandchild

Me

Their birthdays

Where they lived

How I felt going to visit

How often we saw them

Any sleepovers

Any pets

The games we played

The places we went

I am their
eldest/middle/youngest
grandchild

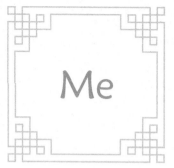

Me

My closest Grandparent

Who I was closest to . . . .

How they made me feel . . . .

. . . .

Jewellery I have of theirs . . . .

. . . .

Keepsakes I have of theirs . . . .

. . . .

Habits to highlight . . . .

. . . .

Cherished hobbies

. . . .

. . . .

Me

What they looked/sounded/dressed like,
their smell, habits & hobbies, how they acted

....

....

....

How they each made me feel ....

....

....

Big savers or big money spenders ....

....

Advice they gave me

....

....

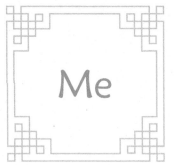

Me

Their cars

....

....

Their party tricks

....

....

Presents they bought

....

....

Illness/accidents/surgery

....

....

Catchphrases & favourite sayings

....

....

....

Me

Special memories with
my Grandparents

My Mum

Her Birth Name

Her Siblings ....

Her Mum ....

Her Dad ....

My Mum's childhood ....

....

My Mum as a Mum ....

....

Keepsakes I have of hers ....

....

What she always wore

....

....

12//52

My Mum

Her birthday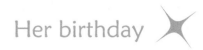

....

Her pride in me

....

Her kindness

....

Illness/accidents/surgery

....

....

Feelings of unconditional love she gave me

....

How she was during her mid life ....

Great advice she gave me ....

....

How we get/got on

....

13//52

....

My Mum

. . . .

Her good friends . . . .

. . . .

Her favourite things to buy . . . .

. . . .

Her work/career . . . .

. . . .

Cigarettes & alcohol . . . .

. . . .

How she best got/gets around: Car, bike, bus
walking, tram, scooter, train

. . . .

. . . .

My Mum

Special memories
with my Mum

My Dad

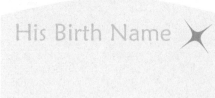

His Birth Name

His Siblings . . . .

His Mum . . . .

His Dad . . . .

My Dad's childhood . . . .

. . . .

My Dad as a Dad . . . .

Keepsakes I have of his . . . .

. . . .

What he always wore

. . . .

. . . .   16/52

My Dad

His birthday

. . . .

His pride in me . . . .

His kindness . . . .

Illness/accidents/surgery . . . .

. . . .

Feelings of unconditional love he gave me . . . . . .

. . . .

How he was during his mid life . . . .

Great advice he gave me . . . .

. . . .

 How we get/got on

. . . .

. . . .

My Dad

· ·

His good friends ·

· ·

His favourite things to buy · · · · · · · · · · · · · · · · · ·

· ·

His work/career ·

· ·

Cigarettes & Alcohol ·

· ·

How he best got/gets around: Car, bike, bus
walking, tram, scooter, train

· ·

· ·

My Dad

Special Memories
with my Dad

All about me

My Childhood

About my birth

Day, Date & Starsign

· ·

Time & Place

· ·

Stories around my birth

· ·

· ·

As a baby

Where I lived

· ·

Who lived with me

· ·

Where I slept

· ·

Favourite Toy

Stories of me as a baby

· ·

· · · · · · · · · · · · · · · · · · · ·

My Childhood

As a toddler

First words & First Steps

· ·

Things I enjoyed

· ·

Cute things I said

· ·

Stories of me as a toddler

· ·

· ·

As a school child

Nursery & Schools

· ·

Favourite Friends

· ·

Terrific Teachers

· ·

Stories from school

· ·

· · · · · · · · · · · · · · · · · · · ·

My Childhood

Special Memories

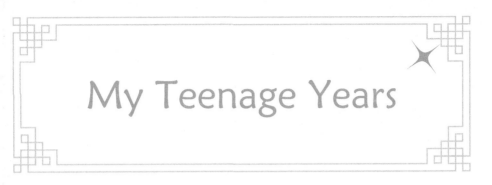

My Teenage Years

13 - 15

Friend group

· ·

Favourite School Subjects

· ·

My Bike/Frisbee/Marbles

· ·

Favourite Dinner/Food

· ·

Cinema/Bowling/Fun days

· ·

My bedroom

· ·

Where we went sledging

· ·

Hobbies/after school activities

· ·

· ·

Favourite Hairstyle & Clothes

· ·

· 23/52

My Teenage Years

16 - 19

Best Mates

. . . .

My 16th

. . . .

Driving instructor/test/first car

. . . .

. . . .

How it felt to leave school

. . . .

School Leavers Celebrations

. . . .

. . . .

Turning 18

. . . .

First 'legal' drink

. . . .

Favourite dancing/nighclub/bar

. . . .

Further Education/

Full time job . . . .

. . . .

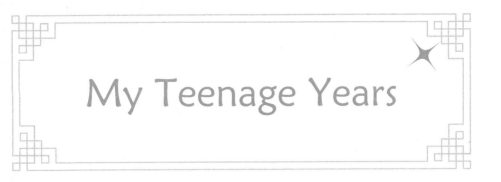

My Teenage Years

Special Memories

My 20's

Happiness in my 20's 🙁 — — — — — 🙂

When I was 21 ....

Graduation/further education/training/work

....

Plans for my future ....

....

How I felt turning 25 ....

What I want my life to be and feel like ......

....

My money mindset ....

How my childhood felt..

Other Memories

....

....

My 30's

Happiness in my 30's

How I felt turning 30 ....

My good friends ....

How my life feels alongside my plans ....

....

How people view me ....

How I view myself ....

Innermost thoughts on my childhood ....

....

Other Memories

....

....

Becoming a Dad

The pregnancy/s ·

· ·

The labour/s ·

· ·

My baby/step/foster/adoptive children · · · · · · · · · ·

· ·

How I felt becoming a Dad · · · · · · · · · · ·

· ·

Tricky Times ·

· ·

Best Bits

· ·

· ·

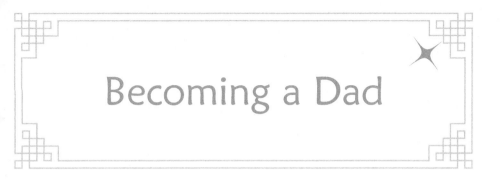

Becoming a Dad

Special memories

My 40's

Happiness in my 40's

How I felt turning 40

My family relationships

What my life feels like

My work/life balance

Turning 45

Any unsettling mid life feelings

How the plans made in my 20's seem

Other Memories

My 50's

Happiness in my 50's

How I felt turning 50 . . . .

How fulfilled I feel . . . .

Hobbies/Gardening . . . .

Important father figure in my childhood . . . . .

. . . .

Illness/accidents/injuries . . . .

How respected I feel as a person . . . .

. . . .

Close family . . . .

Other Memories

. . . .

31/52

. . . .

Being a Dad

What I love most

My hopes & dreams for my children

Important values I set

Times we laughed so hard

Financial advice passed on

Difficult Days

Favourite books we read together

Yearly traditions

Being a Dad

Special Memories

My 60's

How I felt turning 60 . . . .

My good friends & family . . . .

Favourite job I've had . . . .

Thoughts on retirement . . . .

Religious & Spiritual thoughts . . . .

. . . .

Opinion on tattoos & piercings . . . .

. . . .

Looking back at childhood/young adulthood

. . . .

Other Memories

. . . .

. . . . 34/52

My 70's

How I felt turning 70 ....

Stand out friends & family ....

Books that have impacted my life ....

....

Polictics & Fav Prime Minister ....

....

What my life feels like ....

Favourite car I've owned ....

Becoming a Grandfather ....

....

Other Memories

....

....

Space for photos, drawings or more memories

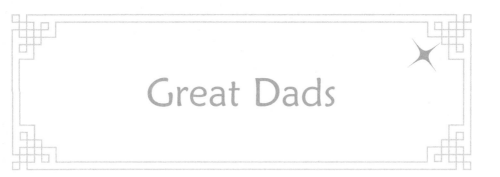

Great Dads

Great Dads I have known

My 80's

How it feels turning 80 ....

Biggest life achievements so far ....

....

How the plans I had for my future seem

....

What I'm grateful for ....

....

Regrets to rectify ....

My mindset around money ....

Favourite Life Experience ....

Thoughts at this stage of my life

....

....

My 90's

How it feels/would feel at 90 ....

People I know in their 90's ....

Memorable world events lived through -
JFK/Aberfan/Moon/Decimalisation/Diana/Wars/Twin Towers/Pandemic etc

....

The kindest moments/people

....

....

How positivity affects life ....

Looking back at my life,
                    how it feels ....

....

....

Space for photos, drawings or more memories

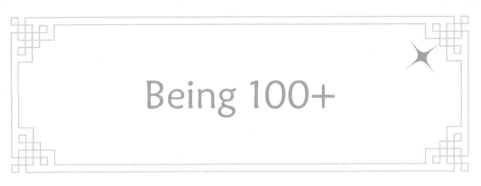

Being 100+

How it feels/would feel at 100 . . . .

People I know that are over 100 . . . .

Feelings around a Royal telegram . . . .

Favourite Royals/Celebrities . . . .

. . . .

How I want to be remembered . . . .

. . . .

Worst decisions I made . . . .

Best decisions of my life . . . .

Advice looking back at my life . . . .

. . . .

. . . .

My Memories

Birthday Treats & Parties

Memories from childhood & as a Dad

Music Memories

Music that means a lot to me

Loves & Marriages

Memories from childhood & as a Dad

Special Sports

Sporting Memories - playing & watching

Christmas Traditions

Memories from childhood & as a Dad

Travels & Trips

Memories from local day trips and far away travels
in childhood & as a Dad

Space for photos, drawings or more memories

Those I have lost

Memories from childhood & as a Dad

Share with others

Share

Advice for a 21 year old

#youdeservetoshine

Share

The impact of childhood

#youdeservetoshine

Share

A memory or secret

#youdeservetoshine

Share

Something I regret

#youdeservetoshine

Share

The best days of my life

#youdeservetoshine

Bring my life, to life

My life comes alive

You have completed these pages for your children, you have shared memories and advice with others and now this book can be brought to life..

..Video yourself reading this book aloud.

Pass on the video when you pass on this book and allow your children to enjoy your stories seeing you tell them, so they can forever more watch what

My Dad Says...

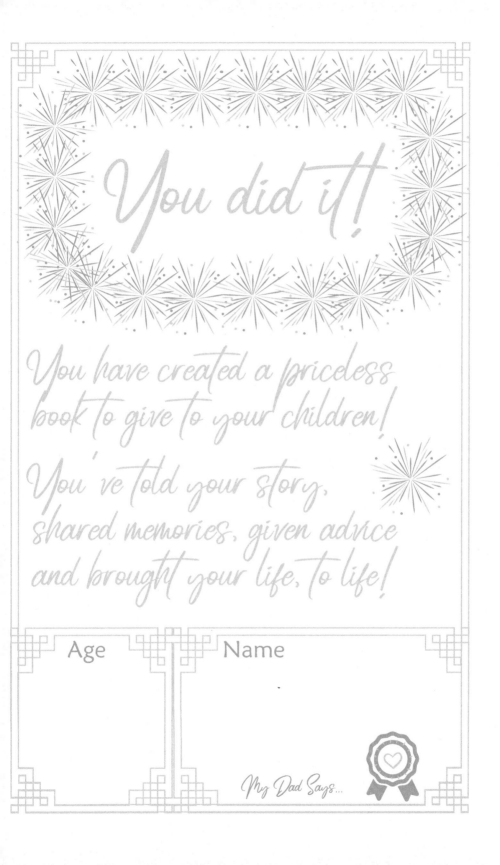

You did it!

You have created a priceless book to give to your children!

You've told your story, shared memories, given advice and brought your life, to life!

Age

Name

My Dad Says...

My Dad Says...

You deserve to shine

'You've got to think positively'

What my Dad says

'Know who is around you, you become
who you surround yourself with'

What my Dad says

'Nurture your children'

What my Dad says

You deserve to shine

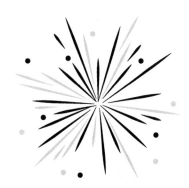

This book also deserves to shine

My Dad Says copying is not cool.

Please do not copy any ideas or wording from this book. Take a moment to think of your own ideas and wording, they can be as amazing as this book is.

Be original,
you do you.

Printed in Great Britain
by Amazon